Space Scientist

GALAXIES
AND QUASARS

Heather Couper and Nigel Henbest

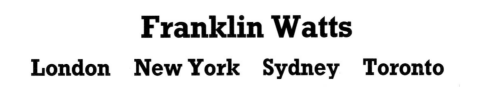

Franklin Watts

London   New York   Sydney   Toronto

© 1986 Franklin Watts

First published in 1986 by
Franklin Watts
12a Golden Square
London W1R 4BA

First published in the USA
by Franklin Watts Inc.
387 Park Avenue South
New York, N.Y. 10016

First published in Australia
by Franklin Watts
Australia
14 Mars Road
Lane Cove, NSW 2066

UK ISBN: 0 86313 473 4
US ISBN: 0-531-10265-3
Library of Congress
Catalog Card No:
 86-50351

Illustrations by
Drawing Attention
Rhoda Burns
Rob Burns
Eagle Artists
Michael Roffe

Photographs by
Science Photo Library

Designed by
David Jefferis

Printed in Belgium

Space Scientist

GALAXIES
AND QUASARS

Contents

Our star city, the Milky Way

Imagine a city with 100 billion inhabitants: a city so vast that a transatlantic jet would take over 100 billion years to cross it, and one so ancient that its history goes back to the time of creation, 15 billion years ago. You and I belong to a city like this – a city made of stars. We call it the Milky Way Galaxy, or just the Galaxy.

All the stars we see in the sky belong to the Galaxy. But even on the clearest night you can only see about 3,000 stars at once. Without a telescope, you're only aware of a tiny fraction of the Galaxy's inhabitants – most of which are just nearby neighbours in our local suburb.

Away from streetlights, though, on the darkest nights of all, you *can* get some idea of the Galaxy's vastness. That's when you can see the Milky Way – a misty, patchy band of light which seems to flow like a pearly river amongst the stars.

Thousands of years ago, people had no idea what it was, and believed it to be made of milk. And yet today, even the smallest pair of binoculars reveals that the Milky Way is composed of incredibly distant stars; stars packed so tightly together they look as if they're touching. But this is just an effect of perspective, a result of our Galaxy's shape. The Galaxy is flattened – shaped a bit like a pair of fried eggs stuck back to back – and we live in the outer "egg-white". When we look around ourselves, into the "white", distant stars seem to line up with each other, and give rise to the appearance of the Milky Way band. Above and below the "white", we look straight past nearby stars into empty space beyond. But the band of the Milky Way is by no means even; there are dark starless patches which were once believed to be holes in the Galaxy.

Living as we do inside the Galaxy – not even near the centre, but about two-thirds of the way out – it's hard to see the wood for the trees. But a bird's-eye view from above would be sensational. Below us would stretch a colossal cosmic catherine wheel, its curving blue studded spiral arms enclosing a golden central hub of stars.

From one side to the other, you would measure its diameter as almost a million million million kilometres. A ray of light, travelling at the speed limit of the Universe – 300,000 km/sec (186,000 mps) – would take 100,000 years to cross it. This means that the Galaxy is 100,000 light years across.

Vast though this distance is, it at least reduces the numbers to ones of manageable proportions. Everything to do with our Galaxy is huge, and many of its stars are far bigger and brighter than our local star, the Sun. And planets – such as those in our Solar System – are absolutely insignificant. If the stars in our Galaxy are like the lights of a city, then their planets, like our own Earth, are no more noticeable than circling moths – dark, small and unimportant.

△ From a bleak pair of worlds far out in the emptiness of intergalactic space, our Milky Way Galaxy would look like a huge starry vortex, slowly wheeling in the blackness. Our Sun (arrowed) – along with its surrounding planets – is just one star among 100 billion, situated way out in the galactic suburbs.

Light years to infinity

Astronomers measure star-distances in terms of the speed of light. Light travels at the speed limit of the Universe – 300,000 km/s

(186,000 mps) – and in one year it covers 9.5 million million km (5.9 million million miles). This distance is called a light year.

Earth's Moon – $1\frac{1}{2}$ light seconds

Sun – 8 light minutes

Pluto – 5 light hours

Within the Solar System, distances can be measured in light minutes or light hours. But most stars are hundreds of light years away.

Nearest star system – 4.2 light years

Inhabitants of the Galaxy

Like a city on the Earth, our Galaxy has inhabitants of all ages. And although most of its inhabitants are stars, it contains other objects too – star clusters, dark gas clouds, glowing nebulae and, almost certainly, millions of planets too small and dark to be seen.

Generally the oldest and youngest inhabitants live in different places in the Galaxy. The oldest stars of all surround the flat disc of the Galaxy in a huge spheroidal halo, which can be traced to 300,000 light years. As well as the ancient red and orange stars scattered throughout the halo, there are over a hundred globular clusters – dense balls of up to a million old stars which sometimes swim through the Galaxy's disc on their elongated orbits. And although the halo *appears* to be very sparsely populated, astronomers now believe that it contains a great deal of dark matter – in a completely unknown form – that is needed to balance the Galaxy's spinning disc.

The halo and the central hub, or nucleus, of our Galaxy – which also contains many old stars – were the first parts to form. This tells us that, billions of years ago, the Galaxy began life as a roughly spherical gas cloud which collapsed under its own gravity. As it collapsed, however, it spun faster and faster, leading to the flattened shape we see today.

The flat disc of our Galaxy is where stars are still being born. Spread throughout the disc is an incredibly thin scattering of gas and sooty dust – millions of times more rarefied than the best vacuum we can produce on Earth – which forms the raw material of future stars and planets.

As the Galaxy spins, faster towards the centre than at the edge, the gas and dust bunch up in a spiral pattern. It collects into huge, black clouds which start to collapse under their own weight. As they collapse, they heat up, and eventually young stars are born inside. These hot, blue young stars shine brilliantly, picking out the spiral arms of the Galaxy like a sprinkling of jewels.

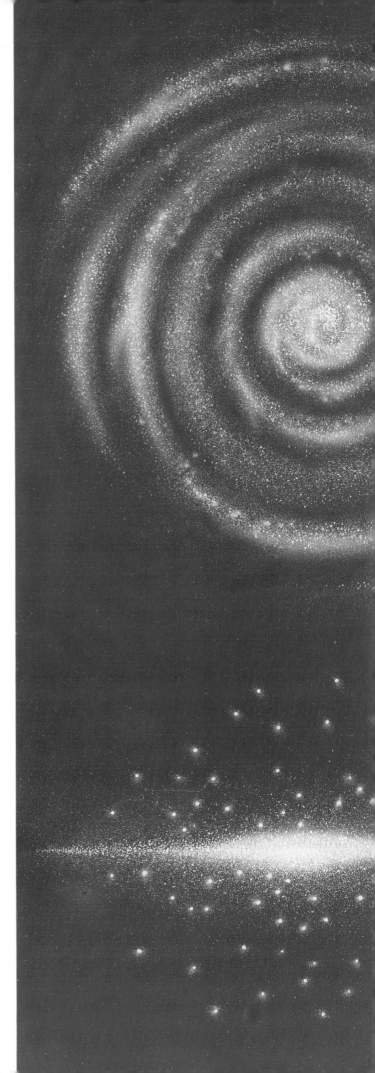

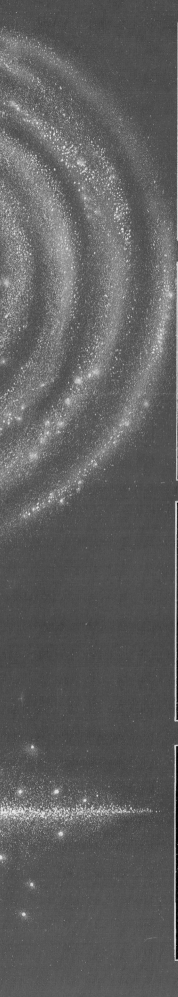

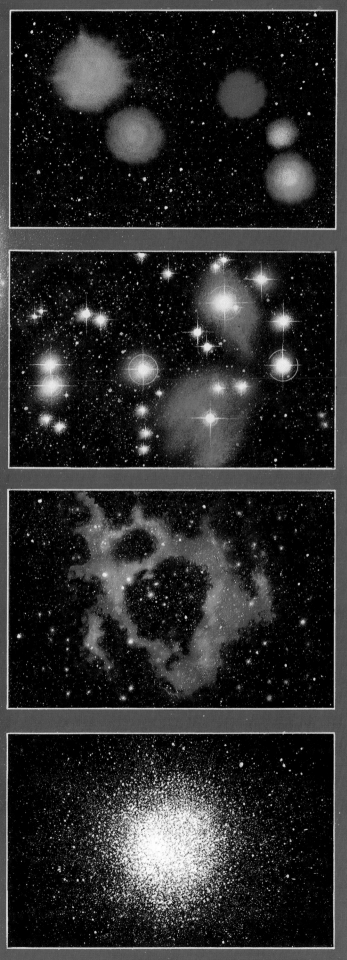

Old stars in Galactic centre

By analyzing the light from a star, astronomers can tell what kind of gas the star is made of, how hot it is, and roughly how old it is. Middle-aged and elderly stars are cool and red. Photographs of the Galaxy's nucleus show clouds of old stars, revealing that this was one of the first regions to be born.

Young stars in spiral arms

By contrast, many young stars are searingly hot, and shine a brilliant blue-white. Like the Pleiades, they're often found in clusters – a result of being born together in a clutch, like eggs in a nest. Only 60 million years old, the 250 stars of the Pleiades are still surrounded by the remains of the cloud that formed them.

Nebula

A nebula, like the Rosette Nebula here, is the most obvious and beautiful sign of recent starbirth. Fierce ultraviolet radiation from the young stars inside excites the surrounding gas cloud to glow, often with a lovely crimson light. The darker regions are concentrations of dust. Like young stars, nebulae are strung out along a galaxy's spiral arms.

Globular cluster

M13 in Hercules – 24,000 light years away, but just visible to the naked eye – is one of over 120 globular clusters which live in the Galaxy's halo. It's a ball of a million ancient red stars, almost three times as old as our Sun. Its stars are packed more than five times more densely than in our neighbourhood.

Types of galaxy

At the beginning of this century many scientists thought that our Galaxy made up the entire Universe. After all, it was unimaginably big, and it contained countless stars. But some astronomers – particularly Edwin Hubble in the United States – became curious about the nature of the many faint, fuzzy blobs they could see in the sky. Some of these were undoubtedly nebulae in our own Galaxy. But others, under the scrutiny of new, powerful telescopes, turned out to be galaxies in their own right. Our Galaxy was just one amongst many.

Today it's estimated that the Universe contains a million million galaxies. Many of them are spiral-shaped, like the Milky Way, but there are other shapes too. The spiral galaxies, though, are the most individual, and our own Galaxy is a typical example – if a bit on the large side. All spirals have a nucleus, or hub, of old

stars, surrounded by a disc rich in dust and gas. Inside the disc, the spiral arms snake their way from the hub to the rim. They're the places where starbirth is most actively underway, and it shows: the arms are dotted with hot young blue stars, glowing nebulae and dark clouds.

Some spirals have a small nucleus and patchy, wide-flung arms; in others, tightly wound arms surround a large, smooth nucleus. Our Milky Way is thought to be between these two extremes, although it's possible that it could be a barred spiral – one whose nucleus is bar-shaped, rather than circular.

Similar to the spirals in their general mix of gas and old and young stars are irregular galaxies. As the name suggests, these galaxies have no particular shape, and they tend to be rather small on the cosmic scale – having fewer than a thousand million stars. Many of them

seem to be forming stars only slowly. Although their oldest stars are as old as in any spiral galaxy, there aren't as many of them – and these little galaxies usually have more in the way of gas reserves to use up.

Elliptical galaxies, though, are completely different. They're made up exclusively of old and middle-aged stars, and their gas reserves are practically nil. It seems that they were very efficient at making nearly all their stars in one go, a long time ago in the past. Unfortunately, this has resulted in all elliptical galaxies ending up as lookalikes! They have very little individuality: each is just a ball of old, red stars. It's true that they range in shape from almost spherical to practically spindle-shaped, but they have nothing of the variety of spiral galaxies.

What they lack in variety, however, elliptical galaxies make up for in their great range in size. The smallest galaxies in the Universe – with less than a million stars each – are elliptical. So, too, are the biggest galaxies of all, which may contain over a million million stars. In fact, ellipticals are probably the most common type of galaxy in the whole Universe.

▽ Ellipticals range from E0 (most circular) to E7 (most elongated); ordinary spirals from Sa (tightly wound arms) to Sc (loosely wound arms), with a similar sequence for barred spirals (SBa to SBc). S0 galaxies resemble the central hubs of spirals, while irregulars form another separate group.

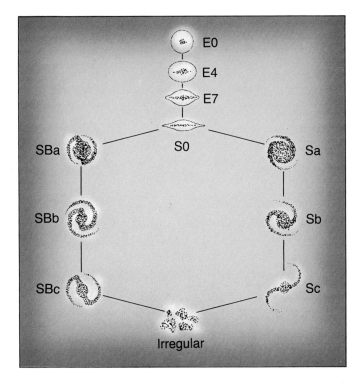

Some nearby galaxies

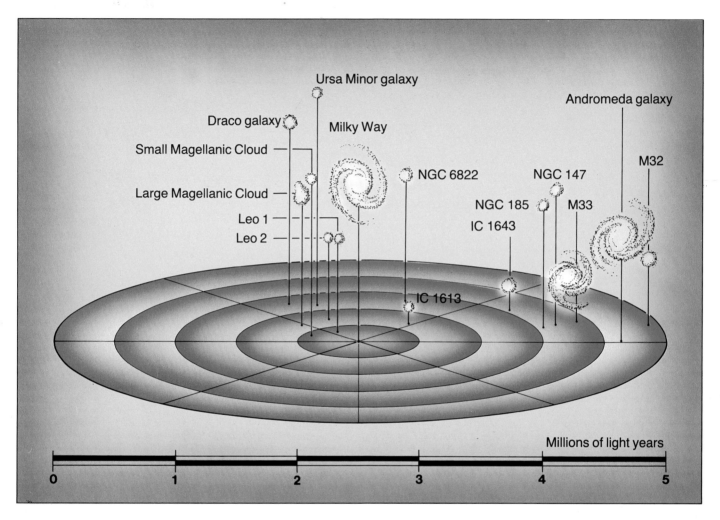

Ursa Minor galaxy

Draco galaxy

Small Magellanic Cloud

Milky Way

Andromeda galaxy

M32

Large Magellanic Cloud

NGC 6822

NGC 147

Leo 1

NGC 185

M33

Leo 2

IC 1643

IC 1613

Millions of light years

0   1   2   3   4   5

Like most galaxies, the Milky Way is a member of a small group, which astronomers call the Local Group. Our Galaxy, the Andromeda galaxy and the Triangulum galaxy M33 are by far and away its largest and most important members. Most of the other 30 or so galaxies in the group are tiny "dwarf galaxies", with only a few million stars each.

The two closest galaxies in the group, the Large and Small Magellanic Clouds, are easily visible in skies south of the equator. They look like detached portions of the Milky Way, but they're independent galaxies in their own right – although it's possible they may be in orbit about our own. In fact, the Small Cloud seems to be distorted by the gravitational pull of our Galaxy and it's possible that it once passed through the Milky Way and was disrupted.

△ The Milky Way, the Andromeda galaxy and the Triangulum galaxy M33 are the largest members of a small group of galaxies called the Local Group. It contains approximately 30 galaxies scattered over a flattened region of space roughly 5 million light years across. The other members are mostly dwarf galaxies.

Both Clouds are irregular galaxies, although the Large Cloud does show slight spiral structure. It is a quarter the size of the Milky Way, and the Small Cloud only a sixth as big. At just 160,000 light years away, the Magellanic Clouds are so close – cosmically speaking! – that we can easily study their individual stars. The Large Cloud, in particular, is a hotbed of starbirth. It contains the Tarantula Nebula, a giant star-forming region almost 1,000 light years across, within which lies a dense cluster of super-massive young stars.

The largest galaxy in the Local Group is not our own, but the Andromeda galaxy. It's almost half as big again as the Milky Way. But although it contains about 300 billion stars, it's so far off – $2\frac{1}{4}$ million light years away – that it just looks like a misty oval patch to the naked eye. In fact, it's the furthest object you can see without optical aid; a staggering 20 million million million kilometres away.

Large telescopes reveal that the Andromeda galaxy is a spiral – probably very similar to the Milky Way. It has a nucleus of old stars, spiral arms studded with hot blue stars and nebulae, and even two companion galaxies. But the inhabitants (if there are any!) of the Andromeda galaxy haven't done so well here; for while our companions, the Magellanic Clouds, are intriguing irregular galaxies, Andromeda's companions, M32 and NGC 205, are small, rather featureless ellipticals.

The third major galaxy in the Local Group is M33, a rather scruffy little spiral which lies quite close to Andromeda. It's only about half the size of the Milky Way, and is still very busy turning gas into stars.

It's not even certain exactly how many galaxies there are in the Local Group. Some are so small that they may have been overlooked. Others may be impossible to pick out if they lie directly behind the densest parts of the band of the Milky Way. Dwarf irregular galaxies, like NGC 6822 and IC 1613, are usually fairly obvious, because they contain bright young stars and glowing nebulae. Dwarf ellipticals, on the other hand, are much harder to spot. Galaxies like Leo 1 and Leo 2 contain only a million stars, the same number as a big globular cluster. But while the stars in a globular cluster are densely packed, those in a dwarf elliptical galaxy are very thinly spread, making the galaxy very dim overall. In fact, dwarf ellipticals are so sparsely populated that if you happened to live on a planet in one, and went out on a dark clear night to look at the stars, you would only be able to count four or five in the whole sky!

Clusters of galaxies

If you have a small or medium-sized telescope, here's something to try in late spring: find the Y-shaped constellation of Virgo – it follows well-known Leo in the sky – and carefully sweep the "bowl" of the Y with your telescope on a low power. You should be able to pick out several smudgy "stars". In fact these are just a few of the 2,000 or so galaxies which make up the Virgo Cluster.

In contrast to little clumps like the Local Group, clusters of galaxies contain hundreds or even thousands of galaxies, swarming together like bees. The biggest clusters of all are roughly spherical in shape and measure about 50 million light years across.

These giant clusters share a great family resemblance. That's because they all contain the same mix of galaxies – mostly elliptical and spheroidal (S0) types, with only a few spirals.

To begin with, they almost certainly contained many spirals; but over billions of years, close encounters between the spirals drove the gas out of them, turning them into bland, gasless spheroidal galaxies. In some clusters, you can see galaxy encounters and collisions going on. The galaxies raise enormous tides in each other, and tear out huge streamers of gas and stars – but the stars themselves are so well separated that they hardly ever collide.

Right at the centre of many big clusters there lurks one supergiant galaxy – a huge elliptical with over a million million stars. Giant ellipticals like this may have got that way through "cannibalism", literally swallowing up other galaxies which swim through the innermost, densest parts of the cluster.

One of the big mysteries about clusters is just how heavy they actually are. In every case, the galaxies moving around inside the cluster swarm much faster than they should. Unless the clusters are all breaking up, which seems unlikely, each cluster must contain hidden mass: about ten times as much as we see in the galaxies themselves. To avoid falling inwards, the galaxies must travel faster against the pull of the "extra" gravity – just as Mercury, closest planet to the Sun, has to orbit it most quickly of all. At the moment, no one knows what form this "missing mass" is in.

Although giant clusters of galaxies are probably the biggest "permanent" structures in the Universe, some clusters group loosely together as superclusters, roughly 200 million light years across. But space isn't filled with galaxies. On the largest scales of all, the Universe looks like an open net – made of huge voids edged with "strings" of galaxies where clusters and superclusters merge together.

▽ The 1,000 elliptical and spheroidal galaxies in the Coma cluster lie 300 million light years away from us, and the cluster measures about 25 million light years across. In this picture the galaxies appear fuzzy, while nearby stars in our own galaxy have sharp outlines and "rays" from telescope reflections.

▷ A fantastic sight in the skies of an alien world within a cluster of galaxies: two spiral galaxies collide, flinging streamers of gas and stars millions of light years into space. Although this galactic pile-up looks catastrophic, actual star collisions are rare – although star-forming gas may be driven away.

Measuring the Universe

So far, we've confidently reeled off distances to galaxies and clusters without a word of explanation. But how do astronomers *know*? The answer is "with great difficulty"! For although it's relatively easy to determine distances to nearby objects, it becomes harder the further you go.

Distances to the nearest stars can be measured by a space-age version of the surveyor's parallax method. When you look at a nearby star from one side of the Earth's orbit – say, in January – and then from the other side, in July, it seems to shift against the background of distant stars. The closer the star, the greater the apparent shift; and knowing the diameter of the Earth's orbit it's possible to calculate the star's distance by straightforward trigonometry.

But stars much more than 300 light years away have parallax shifts too small to measure.

So among these nearby stars astronomers need to identify certain types which can act as "standard candles". These include stars that vary in brightness, supergiant stars and exploding stars (novae and supernovae). All these can be seen at great distances – even in other galaxies – and their apparent dimness, as compared to the nearby "standard", is then a measure of their distance. However, life is seldom that simple! Scattered throughout all galaxies are tiny particles of dust – "cosmic soot" – which also help to dim the starlight. And this is just one of many factors which complicate distance measurements.

Some galaxies are so far away that it's impossible to see their individual stars. But we can still measure how far away they are. Just as you can split up sunlight with a piece of cut glass into all the colours of the rainbow, so you

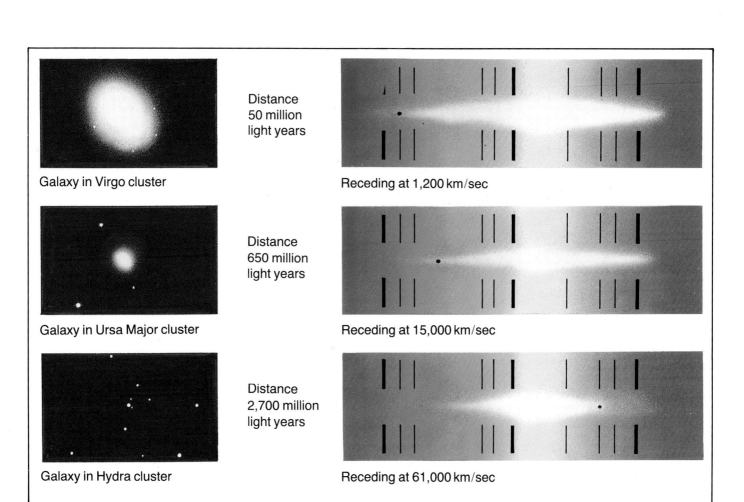

Galaxy in Virgo cluster

Distance 50 million light years

Receding at 1,200 km/sec

Galaxy in Ursa Major cluster

Distance 650 million light years

Receding at 15,000 km/sec

Galaxy in Hydra cluster

Distance 2,700 million light years

Receding at 61,000 km/sec

can split up the total starlight of a distant galaxy with a spectroscope. This way you get a galaxy's spectrum: a band composed of all the colours (or wavelengths) which normally blend together to give the light we see.

Crossing the spectrum are vertical dark lines. These absorption lines correspond to wavelengths where chemicals in the stars' atmospheres have absorbed light, and so tell astronomers of a galaxy's composition.

They also tell you how fast a galaxy is moving. Light from a galaxy travelling towards us seems to have a higher "pitch" – like an approaching siren – and so its absorption lines are shifted towards the blue, short-wavelength end of the spectrum by an amount that depends on the galaxy's speed. Light from receding galaxies is correspondingly "redshifted".

In fact, almost all galaxies show a redshift because the Universe as a whole seems to be expanding. And because it's expanding in a uniform way, the further away a galaxy is, the greater is its redshift. So by measuring redshifts, we can find distances to the furthest galaxies of all.

△ Spectra of three remote galaxies show how the redshift increases with distance. Only nearby galaxies do not have redshifts.

▽ Astronomers use a variety of "standard candles" – stars whose luminosity is known – to measure distances to other galaxies.

"Standard candles"	Can be used to measure up to
RR Lyrae variables	1,400,000 light years
Population II red giants	5,000,000 light years
Cepheid variables	20,000,000 light years
Blue supergiants	80,000,000 light years
Novae	80,000,000 light years
Globular clusters	100,000,000 light years
HII Emission nebulae	300,000,000 light years
Supernovae	500,000,000 light years

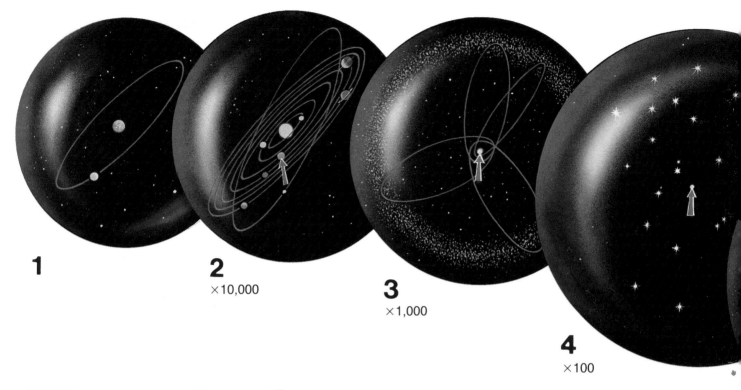

The scale of space

A lot of people are put off astronomy because they can't imagine the vast distances involved. But neither can astronomers! Distances in space are so enormous that no one can possibly get a feel for them. You can appreciate them better, though, by thinking about the *scale* of space – by comparing the distances against one another.

In the "bubbles" on this page, we start at top left with a picture of the Moon going round the Earth. The Moon lies approximately 385,000 km (240,000 miles) away from us, so its orbit measures 770,000 km (480,000 miles) from one side to the other. This is equivalent to just 20 times around the world – a distance an international pilot would have no difficulty covering during his or her lifetime. Remember, too, that the astronauts took only three days to get to the Moon.

The next bubble shows the Solar System. You could fit 10,000 Moon orbits into this bubble – and so, while the Solar System may be small on a cosmic scale, it is huge compared to the kinds of distances we're used to.

Bubble 3 covers a region 1,000 times bigger than bubble 2. However, we have still not left the Solar System! On this scale, we have reached the Oort cloud: the huge shell of comets which is believed to surround the Sun at a distance of a light year or so.

In bubble 4, we reach the stars. In an area 100 times larger than that shown in bubble 3, we see the nearest ones – those within 100 light years. Scaling up by 1,000 to bubble 5, we now see the whole Milky Way Galaxy, 100,000 light years across. A further increase of 1,000 times brings us to bubble 6 and the whole Virgo Supercluster, roughly 200 million light years across. Right in the middle we can see the Milky Way and some of the members of our Local Group – although in reality, the Local Group lies near an edge of the Supercluster.

An increase of only 100 times brings us to the largest scales of all. In bubble 7 we see a representation of the whole Universe, with clusters and superclusters of galaxies arranged in strings, separated by huge voids. In just seven jumps, we have increased our scale 100,000 million million times – or, put another way, that's the number of Moon orbits needed to span the Universe!

From the Moon to the edge of space

1 The Moon's orbit about the Earth, 770,000 km (480,000 miles) across.
2 Orbits of the planets around the Sun, out to 6 billion km (3.73 billion miles).
3 The Oort cloud of comets surrounding the Solar System perhaps a light year distant.

4 The nearest stars, within 100 light years.
5 The Milky Way Galaxy, 100,000 light years across.
6 The Local Supercluster 200 million light years across.
7 Clusters and superclusters cover the Universe, billions of light years in extent.

5
×1,000

6
×1,000

7
×100

Active galaxies

For many years, astronomers looked upon galaxies as placid collections of stars, wheeling gently around in the calm depths of space. But recently it's become clear that many galaxies are in considerable turmoil.

Although "active" galaxies are in the minority – only one or two percent are in any way disturbed – they are fascinating to astronomers. The disturbance is always limited to a tiny crowded region right at an active galaxy's heart, and it represents a tremendous concentration of energy. In some active galaxies, this core is so brilliant that it completely outshines all the billions of stars in the galaxy. Other active galaxies have long jets of extremely fast-moving gas streaming away from their cores. It's a tremendous challenge to astronomers to understand how this colossal energy is produced – and where it comes from.

The first galaxies in which violence was found were called *Seyfert* galaxies (after Carl Seyfert, the astronomer who first investigated them). They're ordinary spiral galaxies like our own, but their appearance is dominated by a dazzling spot of light in their centres. The "spot" – which measures less than a light year across – is surrounded by clouds of very hot gas, moving at speeds of up to 7,000 km/sec (16 million mph)! Astronomers believe the brilliant core is a "cosmic dragon", which excites and energizes the region around it. And there's certainly no shortage of that energy – within that central light year or so, the "dragon" packs the energy equivalent of billions of stars. The energy is thought to come from a region around a gigantic black hole in the middle of the galaxy.

There are other galaxies which bear a close family resemblance to Seyferts. Some look even more obviously disturbed, and M82 – pictured opposite – often used to be described as an "exploding galaxy". But the "spray" of dust and gas around M82's core appears to be streaming *inwards*, not outwards. It seems that instead of exploding, M82 is currently colliding with a huge invisible cloud of gas in space. The gas is pulled by gravity towards the galaxy's dense core, where it is fuelling a sudden rapid burst of star formation. And so the disturbance in M82 – and in other, similar *starburst* galaxies – is due to rapid starbirth, rather than to a single energetic "dragon".

Could our own Galaxy be active? To find out, we need to look at its centre – but that lies 30,000 light years away, and it's dimmed millions of times by intervening dust in space. But radio telescopes show a definite disturbance there, although the activity is much weaker than that seen in Seyfert galaxies.

▽ A radio telescope "photograph" of the innermost 100 light years of our Galaxy shows fast-moving clouds of hot gas and a mysterious central object. It's not yet clear whether our Galaxy has a starburst at its heart or a weak Seyfert-type core: it may actually combine both.

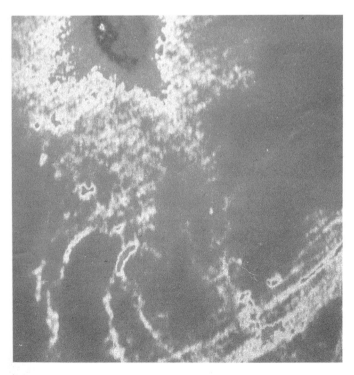

▷ M82 is not an exploding galaxy, but one whose central regions are experiencing a rapid burst of star formation. M87, however, (inset) is undeniably violent. Its most remarkable feature is a jet of gas thousands of light years long, which issues from the galaxy's core at a tenth the speed of light.

Radio galaxies

△ The 64-m (210-ft) diameter telescope of Australia's Parkes Radio Astronomy Observatory in New South Wales studies faint, distant galaxies.

Most normal, inactive galaxies give out energy in the form of starlight. But active galaxies often give out other radiations, too – X-rays, radio waves, infra-red radiation – generated by the powerful disturbances going on inside them. It's only in the past quarter-century that astronomers have had instruments capable of detecting radiations other than light.

Light itself is a vibration of electric and magnetic waves. It's just one of a wide spread of vibrations, which together make up the electromagnetic spectrum. The vibrations all travel at the speed of light, but they differ in their wavelength. Radio waves, for example, vibrate slowly and have long wavelengths, while X-rays vibrate rapidly and have extremely short wavelengths. Light waves, like the middle-C on a piano keyboard, fall near the middle of the spectrum.

Most of these other radiations don't penetrate our atmosphere (fortunately, because some are harmful). But radio waves do. And when astronomers constructed radio telescopes, they discovered that some galaxies – *radio galaxies* – emitted as much energy in radio waves as they did in light.

Radio galaxies are active galaxies which are even more powerful than Seyferts or starburst galaxies. But most of a radio galaxy's energy does not come from the galaxy itself. Instead, it's given out by two enormous radio-emitting clouds – up to a million light years across – which straddle the visible galaxy in space. These clouds are gigantic "bags" of charged atomic particles, protons and electrons. The tiny, negatively charged electrons emit radio waves as they spiral along magnetic field lines in space.

The most detailed radio telescope images today sometimes reveal narrow tubes connecting the clouds to the centre of the visible galaxy. These tubes – which can be millions of light years in length – are like feed-pipes, along which material ejected from the galaxy's core flows into the clouds.

Like all active galaxies, radio galaxies are not "on" for much of the time. Many of them show signs of brief activity, punctuated by long "off" periods lasting hundreds of millions of years. But when a radio galaxy has a fresh outburst, it shoots out jets along almost exactly the same axis as before – which proves that its "dragon" must have a very long memory! And the "dragon" must be very powerful, too, for the jets can apparently move at one-tenth the speed of light.

Radio galaxies are nearly always giant ellipticals. Many supergiant ellipticals at the centre of dense clusters of galaxies are radio galaxies as well. It's possible that their outbursts could be linked to the "cannibalizing" of galaxies which drift too close and pile fresh "fuel" on to the radio galaxy's core.

△ Nearby radio galaxy Centaurus A, photographed with an optical telescope, hides its active core behind a dark swathe of dust.

▽ When Centaurus A is imaged by a radio telescope we see the huge clouds of gas beamed out from the galaxy's active core.

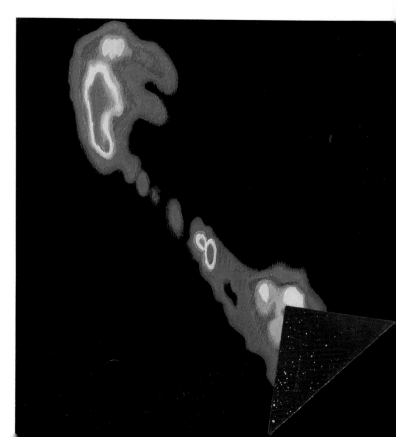

Quasars – the most violent of all

Quasars are the most violent of the active galaxies. And yet no one knew they existed until the early 1960s. It was then that astronomers trying to identify the visible counterparts of strong radio sources noticed that some seemed only to have a faint, blue star in the right position. Stars, however, don't give out strong radio waves – and so the astronomers began to suspect that these objects weren't genuine stars after all. They named the mystery objects "quasi-stellar radio sources", which rapidly got shortened to quasars.

When astronomers analyzed the spectra of quasars, they found that the spectral lines made no sense at all. Then a young Dutch astronomer called Maarten Schmidt stumbled on the right explanation. The quasars' redshifts were so great that completely unfamiliar patterns of lines had been brought into view. Most of the quasars were further than the most distant galaxies – the remotest objects in the Universe.

To be seen at these distances, quasars must be incredibly brilliant. We also know that they're extremely small, because they can change in brightness in a very short time. Like the centre of a Seyfert galaxy, this points to a tremendous concentration of energy. In a quasar, the energy of 100 normal galaxies is packed into a region only the size of our Solar System.

Quasars are probably the super-energetic cores of extremely young galaxies. The core is so dazzling that we often can't see the surrounding

▽ Is this the heart of a quasar? Inside a young collapsing galaxy is a huge central black hole, where gas, dust and torn-up stars spiral to their doom inside a glaring accretion disc. This cosmic vortex acts as a powerful generator, driving shockwaves, jets and gas clouds away from the galaxy's core.

galaxy, and so we're not even sure what kind it is. As it's turned out, most quasars *don't* give out radio waves, so they may live in spiral galaxies.

Because quasars are billions of light years away, we see them not as they are now, but as they were billions of years ago – when they were very young. And it's thought that early on in the life of a young galaxy, some of its collapsing material falls to the centre to form the beginnings of a huge black hole: a region where gravity is so strong that even light can't escape.

Around the black hole, matter swirls in a vortex – the accretion disc – before it is pulled in forever by gravity. Before it vanishes, it glares fiercely as it whips around the black hole's edge at virtually the speed of light. This glaring vortex is what we call a quasar; and it's not content simply to glare. The whirling accretion disc can trigger outbursts, jets – all kinds of violent activity.

A quasar can't last forever. As the black hole becomes starved of infalling gas, its activity dies down. But violence may flare again if the black hole is refuelled. Almost certainly radio galaxies and Seyferts are weak, rekindled quasars.

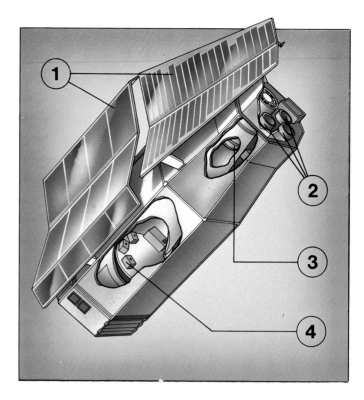

△ The Einstein satellite detected X-rays from quasars: **1** Solar panels **2** Star trackers **3** X-ray telescope **4** X-ray detector

▽ Quasar 3C 273 (photographed in X-rays) is among the nearest quasars. The most distant is 1208 + 1011 at 13 billion light years away.

The expanding Universe

How did the Universe begin? It seems an impossible question to answer – but fortunately we do have a few clues to go on! One is that the Universe is expanding. So what would happen if we "ran the film backwards"? The galaxies would move together instead of separating – until, at a point 15 billion years in the past, they would merge. This is the instant of the Big Bang: the moment of our Universe's birth.

It's impossible to describe the Big Bang. The entire Universe was compressed to a point which exploded with unimaginable fury. The pressures and temperatures were almost infinitely high. Even today, we believe we are picking up the cooled-down radiation from this cosmic holocaust as the *microwave background*. Discovered in 1965, this weak ember is interpreted as further evidence that the Universe really *did* begin in a Big Bang.

▷ Almost certainly, the Universe began in a Big Bang about 15 billion years ago. At the instant of the Big Bang itself, the Universe must have been unimaginably hot and dense, but it has been expanding and cooling ever since. The galaxies formed later, though no one's sure how or when.

Most astronomers accept the Big Bang theory – and they're supported by nuclear physicists, who find that the composition of the Universe matches that which would be expected to follow such a violent birth. But although scientists broadly agree on the details of the Big Bang, the aftermath is a complete mystery.

We know that the Universe must have expanded and cooled: and that gas must have clumped together to form the beginnings of the first galaxies. But no one has seen a galaxy form; our telescopes can't reach far enough away – or back far enough in time. The Hubble Space Telescope, soon to be placed high above Earth's obscuring atmosphere, may give us our first views of galaxy-birth.

It may also tell us about the future of our Universe. Currently, the Universe is expanding, and shows no sign of slowing down. But if there is enough matter in the Universe, its gravity will eventually slow the expansion, halt it and then reverse it – like the elastic skin of a shrinking balloon. In a contracting Universe, our very remote descendants will live in fear of the "Big Crunch", when all the galaxies merge again. However, if you add up all the matter you can see in the Universe, there's nowhere near enough to brake the expansion.

On the face of it, it looks as if the Universe will continue to expand forever, growing colder and emptier as galaxies slowly die. But many astronomers are convinced that the Universe contains huge quantities of invisible matter in an unknown form – perhaps ten times as much as the matter we see. The Space Telescope may give us clues as to where and what this matter is. It may even be able to tell us for certain how our Universe will end.

▽ You can simulate how the Universe expands by painting spots on a balloon, and then blowing the balloon up. As it inflates, each spot moves away from every other spot. The skin between the spots stretches, pushing the spots apart – just as the expansion of space causes the galaxies to separate.

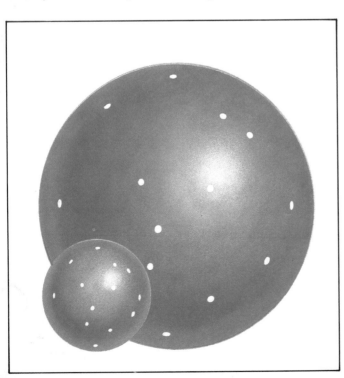

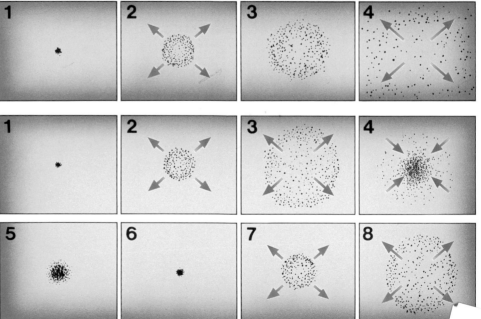

Big Bang – open-ended
The Universe's fate depends on the amount of matter. A "lightweight" Universe starts in a Big Bang (**1** and **2**) and then expands forever (**3** and **4**).

Big Bang – pulsating
If the Universe contains invisible dark matter, then gravity may be able to reverse the expansion. It begins in a Big Bang (**1** and **2**) and expands (**3**), until gravity halts the expansion. The Universe then contracts (**4** and **5**), leading to a Big Crunch (**6**), followed possibly by another Big Bang (**7** and **8**).

The Milky Way Galaxy
– a spotter's guide

Although most galaxies are too far away to be visible, you can explore our own with the unaided eye every clear night. That's when the band of the Milky Way arches across the sky, its stars so tightly packed that they appear to touch. The further you look, the more the stars concentrate into a band. Because we're right inside the Milky Way, all the stars, nebulae and clusters appear piled up on top of each other.

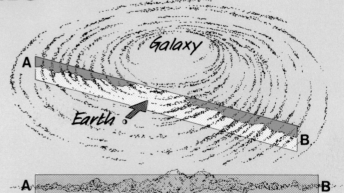

This view is what we see from Earth when we look towards the Galaxy's centre

△ There are hundreds of "open" star clusters in the Milky Way – groups of recently born young stars. If you sweep along the Milky Way with binoculars, particularly through the constellations of Cygnus and Perseus, you'll pick some out.

▷ The Jewel Box, which looks like a misty patch close to Beta Crucis in the constellation of the Southern Cross, is one of the prettiest "open" clusters in the Milky Way. It contains many young blue-white stars and one prominent red giant star.

◁ Journey to the centre of the Galaxy: star clouds in the Scorpius-Sagittarius region billow out towards the galactic nucleus. The tiny, possibly active, core is swathed by heaps of dust. If the dust clouds were not there, we would see the core shining brilliantly.

▽ Even a glance at the Milky Way reveals that it's very patchy in its brightness. This is partly due to our off-centre location within it: stars thin out towards the edge and thicken towards the centre. But most of the patchiness is due to obscuration by dust. These tiny grains of soot create great "holes" in the Milky Way.

△ When you look towards the centre of the Galaxy, you see its most densely populated areas. Enormous star clouds pile on top of each other, while great swathes of dark dust hide other stars completely. For the best views of the Galaxy's centre, you need to travel to the southern hemisphere.

▷ Easily visible to the unaided eye, the Orion Nebula is our nearest star-forming region. The Nebula – in which a cluster of stars has just been born – is a small part of a huge, dark, star-forming cloud extending over the whole of the Orion region.

Galaxy spotting

Even the biggest telescopes don't show galaxies as spectacular whirlpools. Most of the detailed pictures you see in books are long-exposure photographs, which reveal much more than the eye can ever see. Through a small telescope or binoculars, galaxies appear as no more than misty blurs. Here's a selection of the brightest.

▷ In 1845 the Irish Earl of Rosse used his 1.83 m (6 ft) telescope – then the world's biggest – to make this drawing of the "nebula" M51. He suggested, ahead of his time, that it might be made of stars. Compare his excellent sketch with a modern photograph (below).

This direction points to the North Star.

URSA MAJOR the "Great Bear"

M51 – look just below the last star of the bear's "tail"

◁ Galaxies are difficult to find! So use these location maps with a detailed star chart. When you *think* you've found a galaxy, look slightly to one side of it. This "averted vision" technique makes it appear brighter and easier to see.

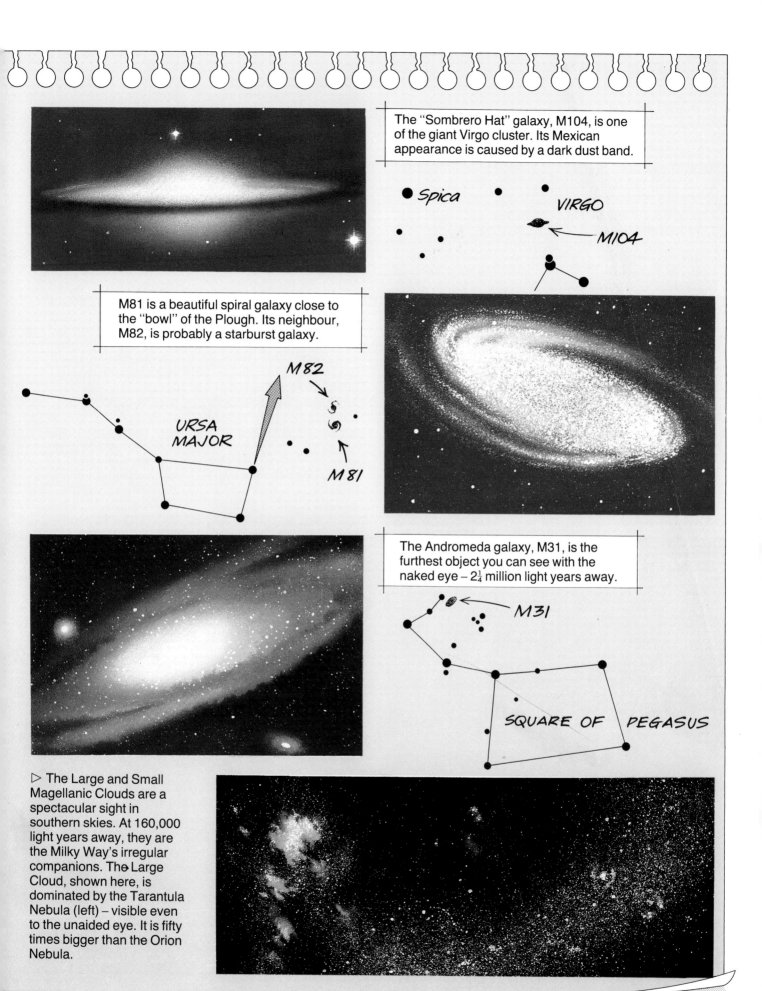

The "Sombrero Hat" galaxy, M104, is one of the giant Virgo cluster. Its Mexican appearance is caused by a dark dust band.

Spica

VIRGO

M104

M81 is a beautiful spiral galaxy close to the "bowl" of the Plough. Its neighbour, M82, is probably a starburst galaxy.

M82

URSA MAJOR

M81

The Andromeda galaxy, M31, is the furthest object you can see with the naked eye – $2\frac{1}{4}$ million light years away.

M31

SQUARE OF PEGASUS

▷ The Large and Small Magellanic Clouds are a spectacular sight in southern skies. At 160,000 light years away, they are the Milky Way's irregular companions. The Large Cloud, shown here, is dominated by the Tarantula Nebula (left) – visible even to the unaided eye. It is fifty times bigger than the Orion Nebula.

Glossary

Atom The smallest part of a substance that can react chemically. Atoms themselves are subdivided into positively charged protons, neutral neutrons and circling negative electrons.

Big Bang The violent event which is believed to have given rise to the origin of the Universe, some 15 billion years in the past.

Big Crunch The ultimate collapse of the Universe which will take place far in the future – but only if there is sufficient density of matter to halt its expansion.

Billion A thousand million: 1,000,000,000 or 10^9.

Black hole A region of space where the pull of gravity is so great that not even light – travelling at 300,000 km/sec (186,000 mps) – can escape.

Core When applied to galaxies, it is the innermost region inside an active galaxy – a zone less than a light year across – where violent activity takes place.

Disc The flat, dish-shaped part of a spiral galaxy in which the spiral arms are embedded.

Dust Tiny grains scattered loosely amongst the "empty" spaces in our Galaxy and in others. They may be a kind of soot blown off the surfaces of cool stars.

Galaxy The Milky Way Galaxy, which is always referred to with a capital G.

galaxy (small g) A collection of millions of stars. Galaxies come in three basic types – *spiral*, which have spiral arms springing from a central nucleus; *elliptical*, which are spherical or ellipsoidal in shape; and *irregular*, which have no well defined shape. Some galaxies, known as *spheroidal* (S0), look a bit like spiral galaxies which haven't developed spiral arms.

Halo A low-density region, made up mainly of old stars and globular clusters, which surrounds most galaxies. However, haloes may contain a lot of dark, unseen matter in an unknown form.

Light year The distance travelled by a ray of light (at a speed of 300,000 km/sec, 186,000 mps) in a year: 9.5 million million km (5.9 million million miles). After the Sun, the nearest star is 4.3 light years away.

Mass The amount of material in a body. On Earth you can measure the mass of a body by how much it weighs; but this isn't true in the low-gravity environment of space.

Microwave background A radio background that is present evenly all over the sky. It is thought to be cooled-down radiation from the Big Bang.

Nebula A glowing gas and dust cloud whose central regions have collapsed under gravity to form new stars.

Nucleus When applied to a galaxy, the central circular hub of a spiral galaxy from which the arms spring.

Parallax The apparent "wobble" that a nearby star shows over the course of a year, caused by the Earth's motion around the Sun. The size of the parallax shift enables astronomers to measure a star's distance.

Quasar A brilliant, tiny object further away than most of the galaxies. Quasars are probably the cores of young active galaxies, whose outer regions are too distant and faint to be easily seen.

Radio galaxy An active galaxy which gives out as much energy in radio waves as it does in light. Most of the radio emission comes from two giant lobes straddling the visible galaxy.

Redshift The shift in the spectral lines of most galaxies towards the red end of the spectrum. The shift is thought to arise from the motion of galaxies as they move apart from one another in an expanding Universe.

Seyfert galaxy A spiral galaxy with a brilliant, active core. It's possible that the Milky Way may once have been a Seyfert galaxy.

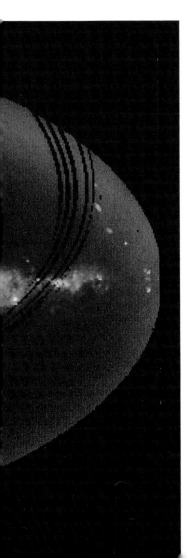

◁ All-sky view from the IRAS infrared satellite, with the band of the Milky Way crossing the centre of the picture. The IRAS cameras registered warm dust and gas and the brightest part of the band is where stars are busily forming. The black streaks are narrow zones not scanned by the satellite.

Solar System The neighbourhood of the Sun and its encircling family of planets: our local corner of the Galaxy.

Spectrum The "rainbow" you see when light is spread out into all the different wavelengths which make it up. You can split up light like this with a *spectroscope*. The word spectrum can also mean the complete spread of radiations making up the *electromagnetic spectrum*, from short-wavelength gamma rays to long-wavelength radio waves.

Starburst galaxy A galaxy with an active core which looks at first sight like a Seyfert galaxy or a quasar. However, the disturbance is probably due to a sudden burst of star formation.

Star cluster A cluster of stars, much smaller than a galaxy. *Open clusters* are loose groups of a few young stars, living among a galaxy's spiral arms; *globular clusters* are dense balls of thousands of old red stars, situated in the halo.

Supercluster A cluster of clusters of galaxies. Most superclusters contain three or four clusters and stretch over 200 million light years of space.

Wavelength The distance between the wavecrests on a train of light waves, or any other electromagnetic radiation (eg radio waves). Short-wavelength radiation is more energetic than radiation of long wavelengths.

Finding out more

Because observatories tend to be located in high, inaccessible places, they are not that easy to visit! But there are plenty of other ways to follow up your interest in stars and galaxies, and one of the best is to join up with an astronomical society.

There are two main societies for amateur astronomers in the UK, and both of these have many members who live abroad. The best for beginners is the *Junior Astronomical Society*. You can get a joining form by writing to Martin Ratcliffe, 10 Swanwick Walk, Tadley, Basingstoke, Hants RG26 6JZ. The *British Astronomical Association* (Burlington House, Piccadilly, London W1V 0NL) caters for amateurs who are more advanced. If you'd rather join a society a bit closer to home, the UK has hundreds of local societies and clubs. There's a new list of these published every year in Patrick Moore's *Yearbook of Astronomy* (Sidgwick & Jackson).

One of the best places to visit for learning more about the stars and galaxies is a planetarium. The main ones in the UK are:
The Armagh Planetarium, College Hill, Armagh, Northern Ireland.
Greenwich Planetarium, National Maritime Museum, Greenwich, London SE10 9NF.
Liverpool Planetarium, Merseyside County Museums, William Brown Street, Liverpool L3 8EN.
The London Planetarium, Marylebone Road, London NW1 5LR.

London Schools Planetarium, Wandsworth School, Sutherland Grove, London SW18.
The Mills Observatory and Planetarium, Balgay Hill, Dundee, Scotland.
Southend Planetarium, Central Museum, Victoria Avenue, Southend, Essex.

There are also museums and observatories open to the public where you can learn more about stars and galaxies. You mustn't miss the UK's two Royal Observatories, which do a great deal of research into galaxies and quasars. They are the Royal Greenwich Observatory, Hertsmonceux Castle, E. Sussex (open in summer), and the Royal Observatory, Blackford Hill, Edinburgh (open all year). For the history of astronomy, there's the Old Royal Observatory at the National Maritime Museum: and if you're interested in radio astronomy, you should pay a visit to Jodrell Bank in Cheshire (where there's also a planetarium). In Australia, you should visit two observatories in New South Wales: the Parkes Radio Observatory, and the Anglo-Australian Observatory.

Index

PRINTED IN BELGIUM BY

proost
INTERNATIONAL BOOK PRODUCTION